FIRST TO FLY

How Wilbur & Orville Wright Invented the Airplane

By Peter Busby • Paintings by David Craig

Diagrams by Jack McMaster
Historical Consultation by Fred E.C. Culick

A MADISON PRESS BOOK
produced for
CROWN PUBLISHERS NEW YORK

PROLOGUE

"Let her go, Orv!"

Young Orville Wright lifted his hand off the little flying toy. The helicopter took off with a whir of flashing blades, shooting straight up in the air. Just missing the gaslight fixture, it crashed into the ceiling, then floated gently down to the floor, ready for the next go.

Orville picked up the toy and handed it to his older brother, Wilbur. The brothers shared all their toys, but this one was special—a helicopter that actually flew. Just a bamboo stick, a rubber band, and at each end, a pair of paper wings. Wilbur wound up the rubber band as tight as he could without breaking it, then let go. As the rubber band released itself, the ends spun around, rotating the wings like the rotors of a real helicopter, and the toy soared into the air.

The "bat," as they called it, was a gift from their father, Bishop Milton Wright. He and his wife, Susan, always encouraged their five children to read and learn about whatever interested them, and the bishop knew how his youngest boys loved anything mechanical. Wilbur and Orville spent hours playing with their helicopter, taking it apart to figure out how it worked and then making another just like it. This one flew, too. The boys would never forget the magic of this special toy.

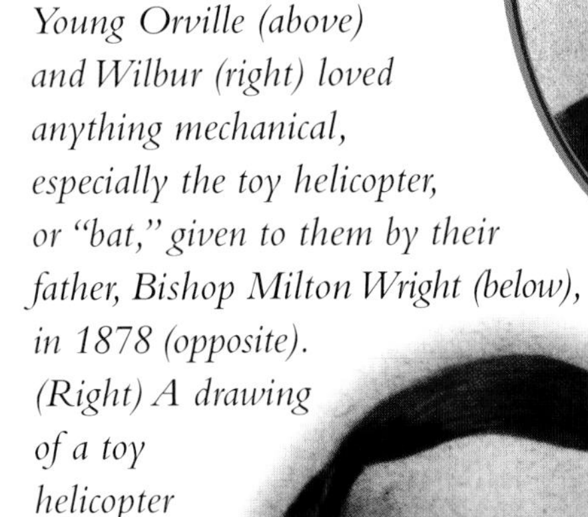

Young Orville (above) and Wilbur (right) loved anything mechanical, especially the toy helicopter, or "bat," given to them by their father, Bishop Milton Wright (below), in 1878 (opposite). (Right) A drawing of a toy helicopter similar to the one the brothers played with.

(Top) The Wright family home on Dayton's Hawthorn Street in 1897. (Above) Katharine Wright, second from the right in this group of her friends, was the only member of the family to graduate from college. (Bottom) Susan Wright was a mother who encouraged curiosity in her children.

THE BICYCLE BOYS

The Wright Cycle Exchange. That was the name on the front of the store the brothers opened in 1892. Later it became the Wright Cycle Company. All across America, young people were taking to the roads, riding this wonderful new invention. The brothers loved cycling. Orville was the racer in the family, winning three contests, while Wilbur preferred it slow and easy, taking long, leisurely rides in the country. He was then twenty-six, four years older than Orville.

The boys had originally been printers by trade, but were well known in Dayton, Ohio, as terrific mechanics. Friends started bringing their broken bikes, asking for help fixing them, and this got the Wrights thinking—why not start our own bicycle business?

Orville and Wilbur (above left and right) had a steady business at the Wright Cycle Company (opposite).

The brothers' mechanical talents came from their mother. Susan Wright was an educated woman, but also very practical. As a child, she used to help her father in his workshop, where he designed carriages and farm wagons. She raised her own children the same way, teaching them to fix household appliances and make toys.

As teenagers, Wilbur and Orville had expected to go to college as their two older brothers had—and as their younger sister, Katharine, would. But things didn't work out that way. When he was seventeen, Wilbur was smashed in the face by a hockey stick. He lost not just his front teeth but also his self-confidence. He dropped out of school and stayed home, helping his father in his church work and nursing his sick mother until she died, in 1889, of tuberculosis.

WRIGHT CYCLE CO

By then, Orville had left school, too. He preferred mechanics to schoolwork and was earning his living as a printer. Wilbur joined him in the business, and together they published two local newspapers and also made and sold printing presses. It was a good living, but not as exciting as bicycles.

In their bicycle store, the brothers sold new bikes and accessories as well as doing repairs. Then in 1896 they started making their own bicycle models.

In addition to bicycles, the first automobiles were appearing on the roads, and the newspapers were full of stories about a new kind of transportation—flying through the air. All sorts of crazy people were jumping off hills "with a wing and a prayer." But there were some serious inventors too, like Samuel Langley, who was secretary of the Smithsonian Institution in Washington, D.C. Langley started by building model planes with steam and gasoline engines. On May 6, 1896, one of his steam-powered models took off from the Potomac River near Washington and managed to stay in the air for ninety seconds before it ran out of fuel and fell into the water—the first flight ever by a heavier-than-air machine with an engine.

That summer, Orville fell sick with typhoid, a disease carried by contaminated water. In those days, one person in four who caught typhoid died, but Orville was strong and lucky. For several weeks, he fought a dangerously high fever before he slowly started to recover. Then Wilbur had some dramatic news for him.

(Top) The Wrights' bicycle shop and its contents are now on display at the Henry Ford Museum in Dearborn, Michigan. (Above) Orville, right, and employee Ed Hines at work in the shop in 1897. (Below) Bicycles put young and old on wheels.

The Bicycle Craze

The second half of the nineteenth century was a great age of invention. Between 1860 and 1900, the forerunners of many objects and machines we use today were first produced, such as box cameras, gramophone records, movies, typewriters, telegrams, telephones, and radio. Towns came to life with electric lights and electric streetcars, automobiles—and bicycles.

The bicycle was not invented all at once. In 1818, a Frenchman built a two-wheeler moved by pushing with the feet, resembling a scooter except the rider could sit and use both legs. The first pedals came in 1839 in machines called "boneshakers," because the iron or wooden wheels made riding so uncomfortable. During the 1870s, bicycles got spokes, steering, brakes, and roller chains. Then, in 1888, a Scotsman named John Dunlop invented the inflatable rubber tire.

By 1890, the "safety bicycle" looked more or less as it does today, and the bicycle industry was ready to take off. That year, 40,000 were sold in the United States. It was the perfect vehicle for young people in cities. Five years later, a thousand companies were producing over a million bicycles a year.

Otto Lilienthal had been killed.

Lilienthal was a German engineer who had studied the problems of flight and tested his ideas by making more than 2,000 flights in gliders that he made from split willow, bamboo, and waxed cotton. On August 9, 1896, Lilienthal took off from a hill near Berlin. Fifty feet (15 m) up, he lost control of the glider and plummeted to the ground, dying of his injuries the following day. His last words, so it was said, were: "Sacrifices must be made."

Lilienthal's daring aviation experiments inspired the brothers, but for the time being they had a fast-growing business to run. In their first five years, they built 300 bicycles in their own workshop. Finally, in the spring of 1899, they were able to take a breather and pursue their new passion for aviation. Wilbur wrote a letter, the most important one of his life. It was to the Smithsonian Institution.

"I have been interested in the problem of mechanical and human flight ever since as a boy I constructed a number of bats of various size. . . . I wish to avail myself of all that is already known and then if possible add my mite to help. . . ."

Otto Lilienthal: The Flying Man

When he was a boy in Germany in the 1860s, Otto Lilienthal was fascinated by birds and the idea of flight. He and his brother made slip-on wings of wood for their arms. They did not work, but Otto did not give up.

Later, as an engineer, he made a scientific study of flight and in 1889 published a book called *Birdflight as the Basis of the Act of Flying.* One of the most important things he noted was that a flying wing needed to be "cambered," or curved like a bird's. Then the air currents could lift the craft off the ground more efficiently. He also made model gliders, but soon realized that the best way to learn about flying was to fly himself.

In 1891, he began making short glides in his backyard. By 1894, he could launch his glider from a hillside and make glides of over 1,100 feet (335 m). He became famous not only in Germany but also in the United States, where he was known to newspaper readers as "the flying man."

Every Sunday, Lilienthal traveled to the mountains north of his home in Berlin and carried his glider to the top of a hill. With its spreading wings, the glider looked like an enormous bat. He stood underneath it with his arms strapped to the wings, holding a bar at the front; then he ran a few steps and launched himself into the air. Soon he was fifty feet (15 m) up, moving forward rapidly while gradually losing height. He kept the glider's balance by vigorously kicking and throwing his legs in different directions to shift his weight. After a few seconds, the glider was almost at ground level. He made a final kick forward, stalling the glider, and let it fall to the earth. The pilot had to be fit and strong to fly this type of glider—now known as a hang glider—and Lilienthal certainly was. He made more than 2,000 flights and was an inspiration to the Wright brothers.

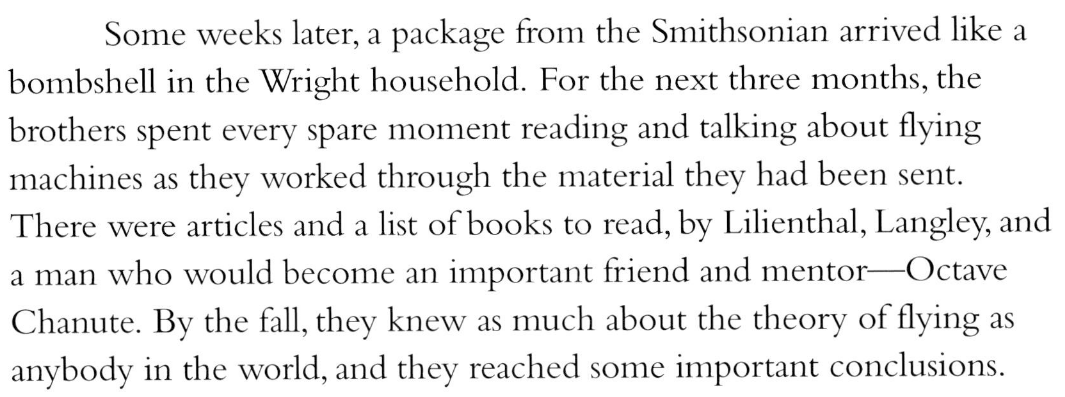

Another flying pioneer was engineer Octave Chanute (bottom), who was born in France but raised in the United States. He wrote Progress in Flying Machines, *a book that the Wrights studied carefully. (Above) Chanute's assistant tests the "double-decker" glider featured in the postcard below.*

Some weeks later, a package from the Smithsonian arrived like a bombshell in the Wright household. For the next three months, the brothers spent every spare moment reading and talking about flying machines as they worked through the material they had been sent. There were articles and a list of books to read, by Lilienthal, Langley, and a man who would become an important friend and mentor—Octave Chanute. By the fall, they knew as much about the theory of flying as anybody in the world, and they reached some important conclusions.

For a plane to fly, the brothers believed, it needed three things: wings to lift it, an engine to move it, and a way of controlling it in the air.

The first two problems had been partly solved. Lilienthal's gliders had wings that supported him in the air, at least for a few seconds. Langley's engine had also gotten the plane off the ground, although without the weight of a pilot. Lilienthal's plane had a pilot but no engine, Langley's an engine but no pilot. The Wright brothers' aim was to have both—a plane powered by an engine and flown by a pilot. But before they could do that, they had to solve the third and most important problem: how to control the plane. The engine, they decided, would come later. To experiment with control, they would first build a glider.

Lilienthal had controlled his glider with his body. The pilot hung below the plane like a parachutist, and by kicking his legs and shifting his weight he tried to steer the machine and keep it balanced. This kind of machine is called a hang glider. But early hang gliders were dangerous, as Lilienthal's death had shown, and this method of control would only work on a small machine. A plane able to support an engine as well as a pilot would need much bigger wings—too large to be controlled by a man hanging underneath. It was obvious to the Wrights that hang gliding was not the solution.

The Wright brothers had one great advantage over other pioneers of aviation: they built bikes. In their well-equipped workshop, they could make virtually all the parts for their aircraft—both wood and metal—at very little cost. Since they were mechanics, the brothers searched for a mechanical solution to the problem of control. Wilbur had observed that birds change the angle and shape of their wings during flight, even twisting their wing tips. Perhaps a plane's wings could be "warped," or

How Does Wing-Warping Work?

As cyclists Wilbur and Orville knew instinctively, when you want to turn a bicycle left, you don't just twist the handlebars, you also lean. They noticed the same thing with birds. When a bird turns, its whole body rolls the same way. Cyclists lean, birds roll—and so should planes. This was the Wrights' big idea. And it set them apart from all other airplane inventors at the time. Amazingly, no one else had thought of this—in fact, Langley, Lilienthal, and Chanute believed the exact opposite. Their machines were designed with wings set at a slight upward angle, which corrected a roll and returned the plane to the horizontal. For them, rolling was dangerous and to be avoided. But the Wrights understood that in order to make a turn, the pilot must also put the plane into a roll—deliberately.

But how? How can the pilot induce a roll and—more important—how can the wings then be brought back to a horizontal position? Once more, the Wrights got their answer from birds. The wings of a bird are not rigid like a piece of wood. They are constantly flapping and flexing and changing their shape. When a bird turns to the left, the tip of its left wing dips and the tip of its right wing rises. Could a plane be made to do the same thing?

Wilbur found the answer in a piece of cardboard. One day in the bicycle workshop, he squeezed opposite corners of a box and noticed when he did so, one corner twisted up and the other down. Could a pair of wings be twisted in the same way?

The brothers built a biplane kite that looked like a box (top). Cords that led to the corners could be pulled to "warp," or twist, the double wings down at one end or the other (right). Wing-warping became part of the control system that the brothers eventually patented. Today, planes have movable flaps based on the Wrights' original theory about flexible wings.

THE 1899 KITE

manipulated, through the use of movable parts to achieve control in the air.

To test this theory, the brothers built a box kite out of wood and cloth. It was five feet (1.5 m) across, with strings attached to each corner leading to opposite ends of a stick. When they pulled at one end of the stick, the left wing would bend downward while the right wing went up. Pulling the other end of the stick did the opposite. Wilbur took this kite out to a nearby field. One day's testing was enough. The kite rolled and turned as they expected. "Wing-warping," as they called it, worked.

The brothers were working on their first full-scale glider, and they needed a place to test it where there was plenty of space, wind—and no one to watch them. Dayton was no good. It wasn't windy enough. Gliders, like kites, need a strong breeze to take off. Wilbur wrote to the U.S. Weather Bureau asking which were the windiest places in the country. The brothers chose the sixth place on the Weather Bureau list—Kitty Hawk, a fishing village on an island off the coast of North Carolina. It was remote and difficult to reach, but it had strong, steady winds and vast expanses of sand dunes—soft places for their glider to land.

KITTY HAWK

(Above) Postmaster Bill Tate and his family on the porch of their home at Kitty Hawk. (Right) The U.S. Life Saving Station at Kill Devil Hills, to the south of Kitty Hawk. The seven members of the station would help the brothers prepare for their flights just like an aircraft ground crew. (Below) Young Tom Tate poses with a prize catch in front of the 1900 glider. (Far right) Wilbur and Orville pitched a tent on the dunes. (Opposite) Wilbur and Orville carry the 1900 glider back to camp.

It was far from perfect, but the brothers would learn to love it. There were two lifesaving stations, a weather bureau, a post office, and about twenty little houses among the sand dunes—but not much else. Wilbur's trip to Kitty Hawk, with the glider packed in a crate, was an incredible journey, by train, ferry, then fishing boat. The last part of Wilbur's trip, in a decrepit, flat-bottomed fishing schooner, was a nightmare. It started off calm enough, but when they reached the open sea, a storm arose. The cabin was so filthy that Wilbur spent the whole night on deck. Soaked to the skin, shivering cold, and ravenously hungry, with nothing to eat but a jar of jam, Wilbur wondered if he'd ever set foot on land again. Finally they docked at Kitty Hawk just before dawn. His hosts—the local postmaster Bill Tate and his wife—greeted him with a splendid breakfast of ham and eggs.

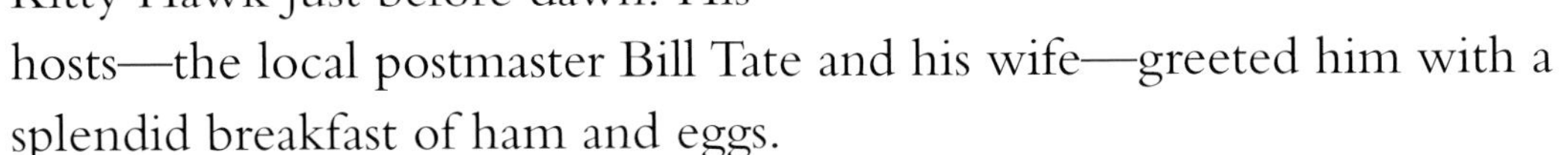

Orville arrived two weeks later, bringing supplies of tea and coffee, and they pitched their tent on the sand dunes, close to where they would fly the glider. Their mechanic, Charles Taylor, was left in charge of the bicycle shop back home.

"We certainly can't complain of the place," Orville wrote to his sister, Katharine. "We came down here for wind and sand, and we have got them." Some nights, when the wind came in from the Atlantic, they would have to jump out of their cots and hold the tent to keep it from blowing away, with sand stinging their hands and faces.

The 1900 Glider

A modern replica of the 1900 glider (top) sits on the beach at Kitty Hawk. The brothers flew their glider mostly as a kite (above). When flown as a glider, the pilot lay flat on his stomach in the middle of the lower wing, his feet resting on a T-bar that controlled the wing-warping. If he pushed the bar with his left leg, wires leading to the wing tips would make the left wing tip angle up and the right wing tip angle down, rolling the plane to the right. Pushing with his right leg would roll the glider to the left. At the front of the glider in the center was the "elevator." It looked like a small wing and, like the wings, it could be warped. The pilot had a hand control that made the rear of the elevator curve slightly up or down, making the glider rise or fall. Controlling the glider was tricky. Once, a gust of wind caught it and slammed it into the sand (above right).

The brothers started off cautiously, flying the glider as a kite. They simply held it up off the sand and let the wind take it, then they played out ropes attached to the struts (the parts between the wings). They pulled on other ropes that moved the wing-warping and elevator (upward and downward movement) controls, practicing keeping the craft level and bringing it safely down to land, learning the skills of a pilot from the ground.

Each flight brought the moment closer when Wilbur would take his life in his hands and pilot the glider himself.

One day in early October, he was ready. He positioned himself in the cockpit of the glider with his hands on the elevator controls and his feet against the wing-warping controls. Orville grasped one wing tip, and Bill Tate the other, and the two hoisted Wilbur and the glider into the air. Wilbur heard a dry crack as the twenty-five-mile (40 km) per hour wind filled the fabric of the wings, and then he felt a sudden weightlessness. Orville and Bill played out the ropes, letting Wilbur soar higher and higher.

The next few seconds passed in a blur. He'd thought there would be all the time in the world to plan his moves, to look around him, and to experience life from the air. Instead he found himself functioning on pure instinct as the plane lurched up and down, one moment plunging straight for the ground, the next nosing upward, threatening to stall and fall over on its back. "Let me down!" he shouted.

Orville and Bill pulled on the ropes and brought the glider safely down onto the sand. Wilbur had done it. He had flown. But he was not intending to risk it again, not until he understood the plane a lot better. For the next two weeks, they went back to testing the craft as a kite, using weights instead of a pilot, noting how it behaved in different wind conditions, and measuring everything: drag, lift, wind speed, and the angle at which the glider kite flew. They even tried turning the glider around, with the elevator in the rear.

In the final week, Wilbur had the confidence to fly again and this time he would try free flight, without the ropes. Altogether, he made about a dozen glides between 200 feet (61 m) and 300 feet (91 m) in length. On October 23, they went home, leaving the glider behind on the

dunes. During the winter, it would be destroyed by the savage Atlantic gales—all except for the sateen wing covering. A few days after they left, Mrs. Tate removed the material and made it into dresses for her daughters.

Next July, the brothers were back in Kitty Hawk with a new glider, twice as big as the 1900 model. They made camp at the foot of Kill Devil Hills, a group of huge sand dunes four miles (6.5 km) to the south of Kitty Hawk. They built a shed for the glider, where they could sleep at night and be sheltered from the punishing weather—either the pounding rain or the scorching sun.

Then there were the mosquitoes. "The sand and grass and trees and hills and everything were covered with them," Orville wrote to Katharine. "They chewed us right through our underwear and socks. Lumps began swelling all over my body like hen's eggs." They tried everything to protect themselves—blankets, netting, and finally smoking the mosquitoes out by burning old tree stumps.

At first the glider performed poorly, but after making adjustments to the elevator and the camber (the upward curve from the front to the rear of the wings), they started doing better. Their friend Octave Chanute was present for their best glide—390 feet (119 m) in 17 seconds. He was impressed, but the brothers were dissatisfied. The glider's lift was not much better than last year, and the controls seemed worse.

(Top left) Orville poses proudly beside the 1901 glider. (Top right) The gliders were always tested as kites before Wilbur attempted a free glide (bottom). (Below) With Wilbur at the controls, Bill and Dan Tate let the wind lift the new glider off the top of the dunes.

On August 9, when Wilbur tried to turn the glider, he crashed nose-first into the ground, banging his head against a wooden strut.

The accident was not serious, but it added to the brothers' frustration, and they left Kitty Hawk earlier than planned. On the train home, Orville said what both of them were feeling: "Not within a thousand years will man ever fly."

The brothers did not stay depressed for long. Instead they decided to go back to the beginning and think through everything they had done. If size alone hadn't improved their performance, then maybe the secret was the shape of the glider and the wings. To research this, they built a wind tunnel in the workshop. For the next few months, there would be no camping on the dunes and gliding in the open air. Instead they were indoors, testing almost two hundred wing shapes. Every day, they made new discoveries about how the wings of a plane behave in the air. At the end of their research, they had the design of a new glider that was very different from the ones they had made before.

In the first three days back at Kitty Hawk, they made more than fifty flights in the 1902 glider. Already they were staying in the air longer than they had before. Orville had begun to fly a little in the previous year, and now he was making half the flights. One day, as he took the plane higher, the glider nosed upward at a dangerous angle. Orville pushed on the elevator, struggling to get the plane level again. To his horror, he found himself slipping backward, tail-first, toward the ground. There was a crash of splintering timber as the tail pounded into the sand.

Orville stepped out of the glider without a scratch. The tail could soon be mended, but it was obvious there was something wrong with its design. The 1902 glider was their first one to have a tail, which was fixed in a vertical position. The tail was supposed to give the plane more control, but Orville felt it wasn't doing that. He had an idea. What if they put a hinge on the tail, so that the pilot could move it at the same time as he warped the wings to make a turn?

The Wright Wind Tunnel

A wind tunnel is a long box, open at one end with a fan at the other. The fan pushes air through the box. Models are placed inside so you can see how they behave in a current of air, and this tells you how a full-size object would react in real life. Nowadays, engineers use giant wind tunnels to test aircraft, like the Wright *Flyer* replica at NASA (left), as well as cars and trains. A hundred years ago, wind tunnels were rare.

The Wrights' wind tunnel (opposite) was six feet (1.8 m) long by two feet (.6 m) across, with a glass panel in the top so they could see what was happening inside. The fan blew air through the tunnel at 27 miles (43 km) per hour. They made little models of wings, in different shapes and sizes, and measured the lift and drag produced by each one. They tested almost two hundred kinds of wing, looking for the perfect shape—the one that would give them the most lift and the least drag. When they finished, they built their 1902 glider based on their findings.

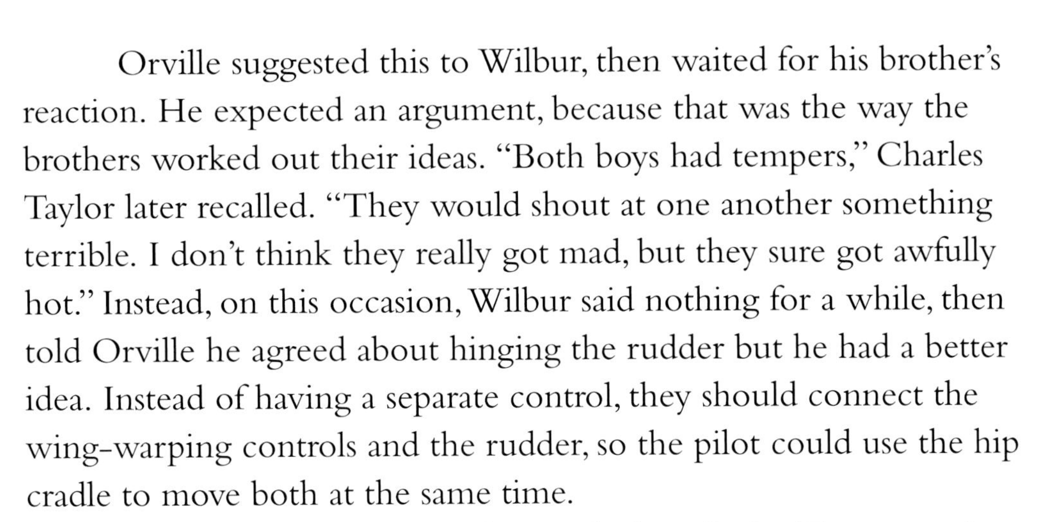

The 1902 glider (left) was their first one with a fixed tail. After problems during early trials, Orville suggested a movable tail or rudder. (Below) With a rudder, they could keep the glider pointed in the proper direction as they rolled into a turn.

Orville suggested this to Wilbur, then waited for his brother's reaction. He expected an argument, because that was the way the brothers worked out their ideas. "Both boys had tempers," Charles Taylor later recalled. "They would shout at one another something terrible. I don't think they really got mad, but they sure got awfully hot." Instead, on this occasion, Wilbur said nothing for a while, then told Orville he agreed about hinging the rudder but he had a better idea. Instead of having a separate control, they should connect the wing-warping controls and the rudder, so the pilot could use the hip cradle to move both at the same time.

That's what they did, and it worked perfectly. They started doing longer glides, and the control problem was solved.

That year, the Wright brothers made almost a thousand flights. On their final day of gliding, they broke their record again with a glide of 622 feet (190 m), lasting 26 seconds. Wilbur and Orville went home happy. They had achieved their first goal, designing a glider that could be controlled in the air. Now they were ready to build a plane with an engine and propellers.

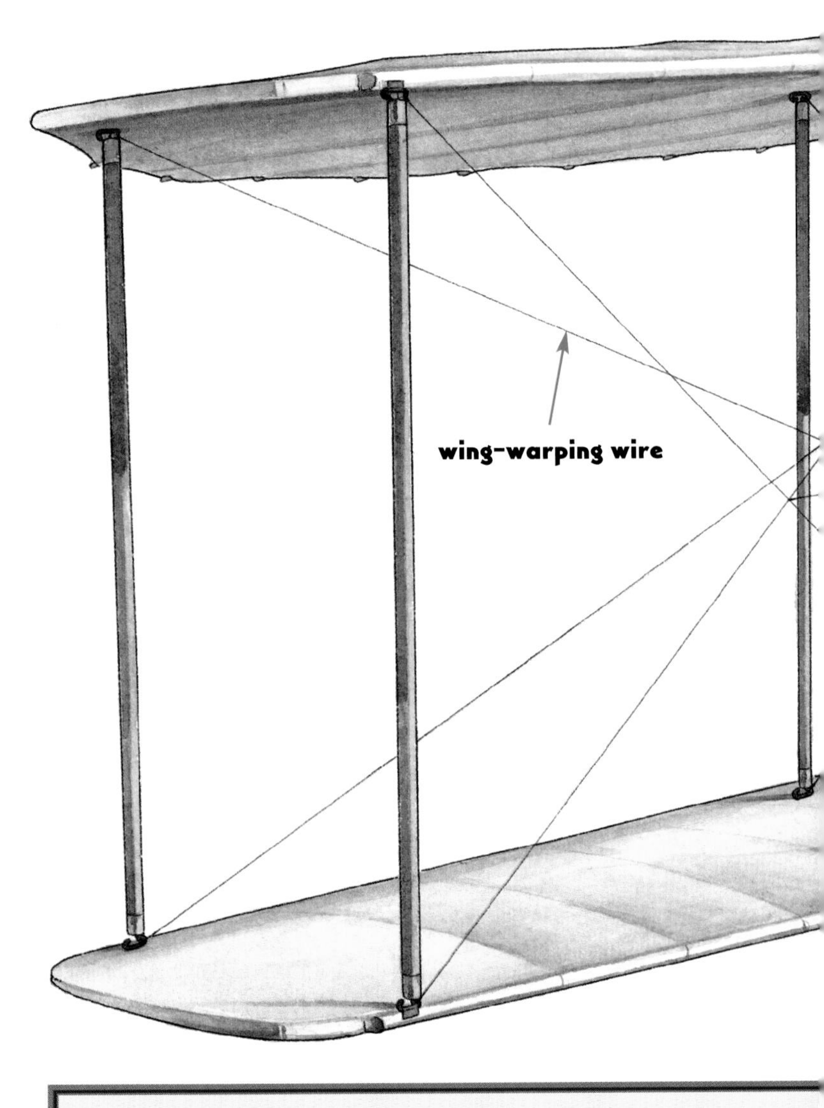

The 1903 Wright Flyer

The plane the brothers worked on in the fall of 1902 and into 1903 was built of spruce, braced with wire, and covered with muslin. The pilot lay on the lower wing beside the engine. With his left hand, he could control the twin elevators and make the plane climb or descend. In the wing-warping cradle, he twisted his hips to control wires connected to the wing tips and rudders. The two rudders helped control side-to-side movement (yaw). The 12-horsepower engine that the Wrights built used gasoline as fuel. It was mounted to the side to balance the pilot's weight.

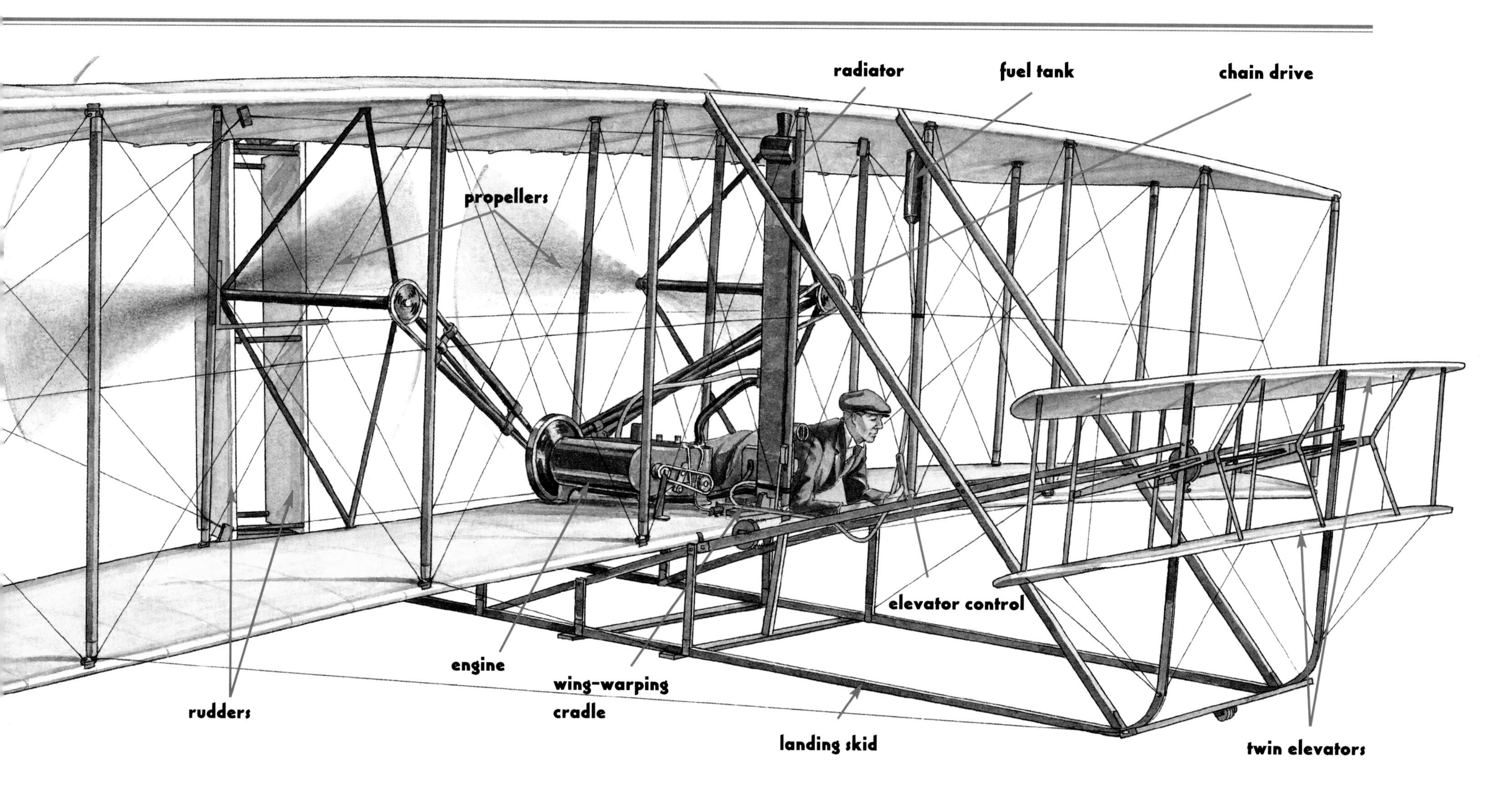

A water-filled **radiator** cooled the engine. The brothers designed their own propeller made of wood. There were two **propellers**, one for each wing, powered by **chain drives** from the engine, one rotating clockwise and the other counterclockwise. The propellers provided thrust—pushing the plane forward.

The Wrights achieved what others had failed to—controlled flight—because their *Flyer* was the first plane to coordinate the three movements of all aircraft.

Pitch. The up or down movement of the nose of a plane—as if the plane were rotating around an axis running through the wings.

Roll. The movement of one wing up while the other moves down—as if the wings were rotating around an axis running the length of the plane. Also called banking.

Yaw. The movement of a plane's nose from side to side—as if the plane were rotating around an axis running from the top to the bottom.

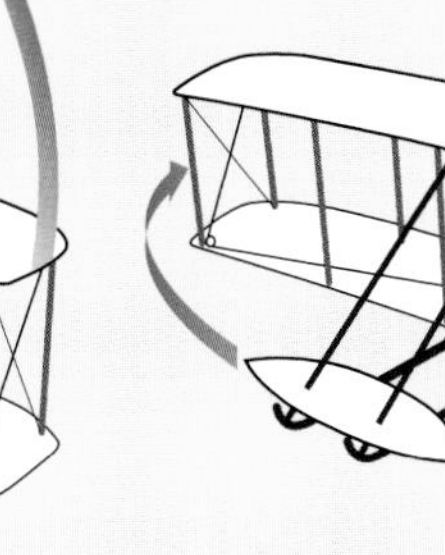

TWELVE MAGIC SECONDS

On the morning of December 17, 1903, Wilbur and Orville Wright stepped out of their shack and looked around them. Ice had formed in puddles between the sand dunes from the heavy rain overnight, but the sky was now clear. The weather was almost perfect—except for the wind.

The winds were stiff today—thirty knots. The brothers were cautious men. Any other day they would have waited for calmer conditions, but they had lost enough time already in the two months they'd spent at Kitty Hawk. There had been problems tuning the engine, making it run smoothly, and cranking up the power, and twice they had had to send the propeller shafts back to Dayton for repairs. Soon it would be winter, the weather would be too harsh, and they'd have to get back home to the bicycle shop.

They decided to risk it. Today was the day.

(Above) Wilbur and Orville's ground crew, two children, and a dog stand by as the Flyer *sits on the track on Kill Devil Hills before the attempted flight on December 14, 1903. (Opposite) Wilbur and Orville start their engine by spinning the blades of the two propellers.*

They were going to attempt to fly their plane.

Orville hoisted a large red flag on the roof of the shack. The flag was a signal to the men of the Kill Devil Life Saving Station, a mile (1.6 km) away, to come and lend a hand. The over 700-pound (318-kg) *Flyer* was too heavy for two men to carry by themselves. And the brothers had another reason for inviting people to join them. If the world was going to believe them, they had to have witnesses.

A short distance from the house, Wilbur and Orville started laying a line of wooden beams. The machine would move along this track until the propellers pushed the wings through the air fast enough to lift the plane off the ground. By the time they'd finished, the lifesaving crew had arrived.

Once the *Flyer* was in position, Wilbur and Orville took hold of the blades of the two propellers and pulled hard to give them a spin. The engine sputtered and coughed into life.

Wilbur took aside one of the lifesavers, John Daniels, and showed him the camera placed on a tripod near the ramp. There was a cord attached to it with a rubber ball at the end. When the *Flyer* leaves the ground, Wilbur explained, you squeeze this ball. Daniels looked worried. He had never used a camera before.

The two brothers walked away from the others for a quiet moment. They had spent five years on this project, designing a series of gliders, learning how to control them in the air, and finally, because no one else could make an engine light enough and powerful enough, they had built one themselves in the bicycle workshop.

They had made their first attempt with the Wright *Flyer* three days earlier, on December 14. The track was laid down the side of a hill; then the brothers tossed a coin to decide who would be the pilot. Wilbur won. He climbed into the plane. The *Flyer* rattled down the ramp and lifted off. Wilbur was in the air—but soon he was in trouble. He rose no higher than fifteen feet (4.6 m), then lost height, landing awkwardly with the left wing plowing into the sand. Some might call this a flight, but not the Wrights. A flight for them had to be controlled.

The *Flyer* was soon repaired. It was a mistake, the brothers decided, to take off going downhill. Today they had laid the track on a flat piece of sand.

Now it was Orville's turn to be the pilot. He climbed into the hip cradle on the bottom wing and lay flat on his stomach, settling his hips into the cradle that controlled the wing-warping and rudder, and grasping the lever that controlled the elevator.

"Orville's going to be nervous," Wilbur said to the men watching. "Let's try and cheer him on. Holler and clap."

He turned back to his brother and they clasped hands as if, one of the lifesavers said later, "they weren't sure they'd ever see each other again."

Wilbur took his place at the wing tip as his brother released the wire holding the straining plane in place. The propellers began to move the plane faster and faster along the track.

Wilbur was running next to him, shouting encouragement, ready to let go of the wing.

Then, forty feet (12 m) down the track, the *Flyer* lifted into the air.

Wilbur clicked on his stopwatch.

Orville pulled back on the elevator. The *Flyer* started up at a dangerous angle, about to stall and fall back on its tail. Orville reacted, throwing the elevator lever down. Now the *Flyer* was heading for the ground. Another touch on the elevator pulled the plane up again.

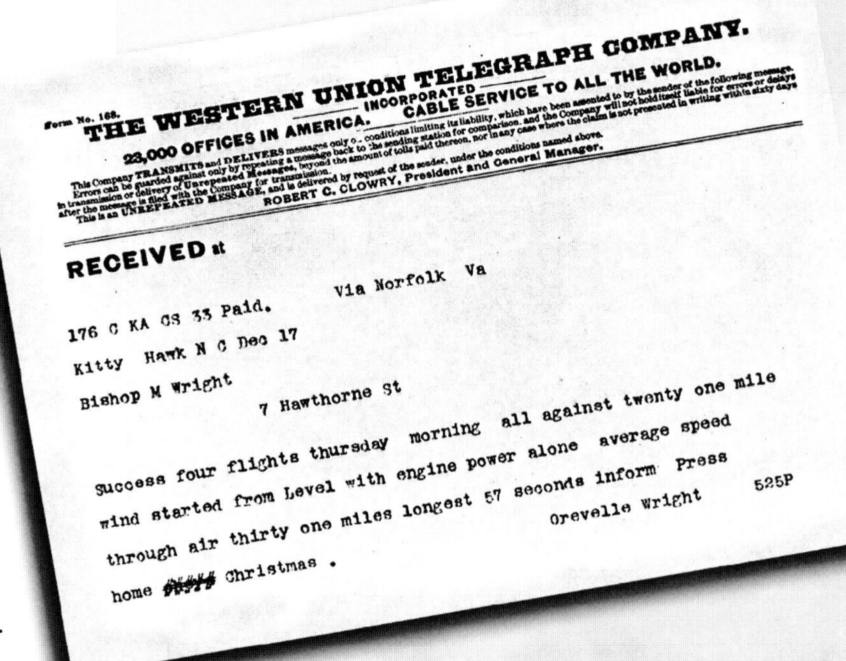

Form No. 168.
THE WESTERN UNION TELEGRAPH COMPANY.
INCORPORATED
23,000 OFFICES IN AMERICA. CABLE SERVICE TO ALL THE WORLD.
ROBERT C. CLOWRY, President and General Manager.

RECEIVED at

176 C KA CS 33 Paid. Via Norfolk Va
Kitty Hawk N C Dec 17
Bishop M Wright
7 Hawthorne St
Success four flights thursday morning all against twenty one mile wind started from Level with engine power alone average speed through air thirty one miles longest 57 seconds inform Press home Christmas . Orevelle Wright 525P

(Below) At Kill Devil Hills, at 10:35 A.M., December 17, 1903, Orville takes off on the first-ever manned and powered flight. Wilbur, who steadied the plane while it moved down the launching rail, is still half running. This famous photograph was taken with Orville's camera by John Daniels, one of the lifesaving station crew. (Above) The triumphant telegram that the brothers sent home contained two errors: the longest flight was misreported at 57 seconds instead of 59 and Orville's name was misspelled.

Then down, and the *Flyer* pancaked into the ground. It was a hard landing, but both the plane and the pilot were in one piece.

Wilbur stopped his watch. The *Flyer* had been in the air for twelve seconds. He turned to John Daniels. "Did you get it?"

He had. His picture of the *Flyer* three feet (.9 m) off the ground, with Orville on board and Wilbur running beside him, is one of the most famous photographs ever taken.

Orville had flown 120 feet (36.5 m). Both of them thought they could do better. At 11:20 A.M., Wilbur made a flight of 175 feet (53 m). Then it was Orville's turn again. He managed 200 feet (61 m). At noon, Wilbur climbed into the pilot's cradle. For the first 300 feet (91 m), it was like the other flights, with the plane bouncing up and down. Then Wilbur managed to keep it level for another 500 feet (152 m) until a sudden gust of wind caught it, sending it diving toward the ground.

Wilbur stepped out of the cradle, unhurt. He had flown for 59 seconds, traveling 852 feet (260 m).

Once again, the seven men started back to the track carrying the plane. Just as they reached the track and set the machine down, the wind rose suddenly and caught the *Flyer*. Everyone jumped for it, John Daniels getting tangled in the wires as the plane rolled over and over. When it finally came to rest, the others rushed up and cut him free, snapping a few more wires and wooden ribs as they did so. He was lifted out uninjured.

The *Flyer* was smashed to pieces—but no matter. The Wrights were already thinking ahead, to their next and even *better* plane.

"They done it! They done it! Damn'd if they ain't flew!"

One of the young men had dashed all the way to the post office at Kitty Hawk to deliver the news. For the Wright family it took a while longer, until the telegram arrived at 5:30 that evening. "Success four flights Thursday morning," it read. "All against twenty-one-mile wind started from level with engine power alone, average speed through air thirty-one miles, longest 59 seconds. Inform press. Home Christmas. Orville Wright."

BROTHERS in FLIGHT

Bishop Wright did inform the press, but hardly any newspapers were interested. Reporters had heard it all before—people claiming they could fly—and who were these Wright brothers anyway? Just two ordinary guys from the Midwest, bicycle-makers who had never even attended college. The Wright brothers didn't mind this at all. They much preferred to be left alone to develop their invention in private; they were worried that someone would steal their ideas.

They applied for a patent (a legal document that states who is the owner of an invention) while continuing to work on a plane that would stay up longer and be controlled more easily. Now that they had a working engine, wind was less important, and they were able to carry out their experiments nearer home, in a hundred-acre field close to Dayton called Huffman Prairie.

They devised a simple catapult to help them take off. A weight, dropping from the top of a tower, tugged on a rope and pulled the *Flyer* along the track, helping it reach flying speed. In the next two years they built two more *Flyers*, improving the engine, the propellers, the controls, and the wings. They learned to make complete turns around the field and do figure eights. On October 5, 1905, Wilbur made the first long distance flight, traveling 24 miles (38 km) and staying up for 38 minutes, landing only when the gasoline ran out.

In 1906, their patent was granted. They were now ready to show their *Flyer* to the world. The United States Army made them an offer. If the Wrights could produce a plane that would fly 125 miles (201 km) at a speed of 40 miles (64 km) per hour, and stay in the air for over an hour, the Army would buy it for $25,000. Some French businessmen also agreed to buy a plane. The brothers started making two new planes,

(Opposite) The brothers made several successful flights at Kitty Hawk before moving their base to Huffman Prairie, near Dayton. (Above) The brothers applied in 1903 for a patent for the wing-warping theory used in the 1902 glider. It was granted in 1906. (Left) Now seated at the controls—rather than lying flat—Wilbur poses for the camera. (Below) Wilbur adjusts the engine before takeoff. (Bottom) Volunteers pull the rope that lifts a weight inside a tower. The Flyer *now uses the dropping weight to catapult it down the track.*

(Above) In August 1908, Wilbur amazed the crowd at Le Mans, France, with his effortless flying. He became an instant celebrity in the French press, as shown in this picture magazine. "We are as children compared with the Wrights," said one French aviator. (Opposite) During a military test flight by Orville at Fort Myer, a propeller blade broke, causing the plane to crash. Orville was seriously injured and his passenger, Lieutenant Thomas Selfridge, was killed.

their first with seats for the pilot and a passenger. Orville would take one of them to Fort Myer, near Washington, D.C., to demonstrate to the Army, while the other would be flown by Wilbur in France.

In the four years since the Wrights' first flight, two Frenchmen had also succeeded in flying. The French press ridiculed the Wright brothers, calling them "bicycle peddlers" and "bluffers." Wilbur had something to prove, and on August 8, 1908, at Le Mans, a hundred miles (161 km) southwest of Paris, he got his chance.

Wilbur was in the air less than two minutes, but what a flight it was. He circled the field twice, rolling the plane with each turn, showing an ease and control that was far beyond anything seen in Europe. "Well, we are beaten," admitted one French flyer. The crowd was small that first day, but word spread quickly, and within a few days the *Flyer* was performing in front of thousands. "I've seen him," exclaimed the newspaper *Le Figaro*. "Yes! I have today seen Wilbur Wright and his great white bird."

In the United States, Orville was wowing the spectators, too. On September 10, he surpassed the Army's conditions with a flight of seventy minutes. He also had to prove that the *Flyer* could carry a passenger.

Orville made several such flights successfully. Then on September 17, he took off with a young officer, Lieutenant Thomas Selfridge, in the passenger's seat. All went well at first. Orville circled the field four times at a height of 150 feet (46 m), but in the middle of the fifth circuit he heard some thumps behind him, and the plane started pulling to the right. Orville immediately turned off the engine, hoping to glide the plane back to the ground. But he was already too late. A propeller blade had split, severing a rudder wire and forcing the plane into a nosedive. Orville frantically pulled at the levers, warping the wings, trying to lift the elevator. Nothing worked. The plane no longer responded to the controls. "Oh! Oh!" Selfridge cried. The *Flyer* crashed into the ground at a steep angle, splitting wood and shredding fabric.

The two men were dragged out of the wreckage and rushed to the hospital. Surgeons struggled to save Selfridge's life, but their efforts were in vain. He died that evening, the first person ever to be killed in a powered airplane. Orville was badly hurt, with scalp wounds, broken hip and ribs, and a back injury that would pain him the rest of his life.

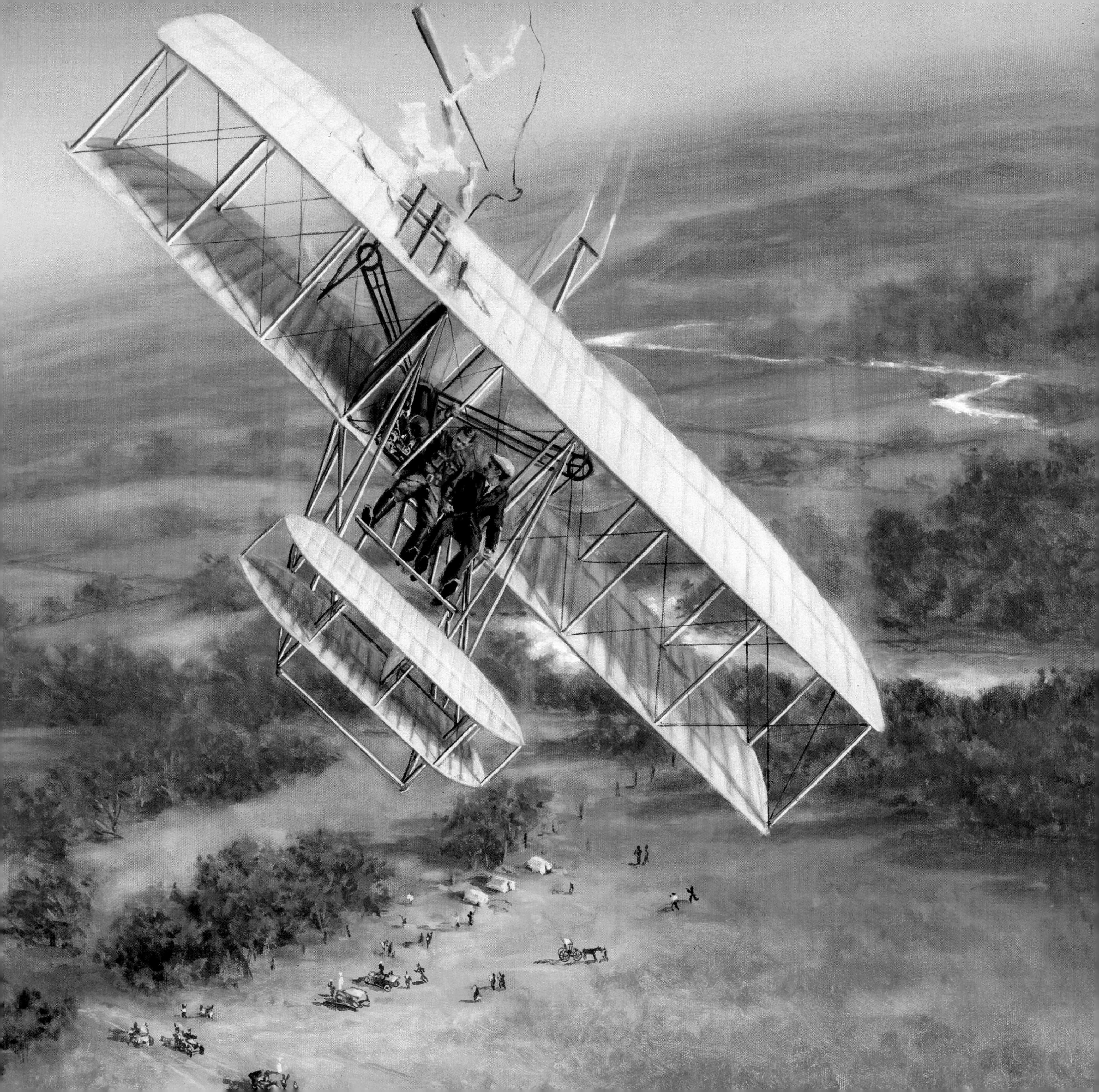

(Above) A German postcard features a cartoon of Wilbur at the controls of the Flyer. *(Below left) Crowds gather at the Hawthorn Street house to greet the Wrights on their return to America. (Below right) The homecoming celebration in May 1909 included parades, festive banners, and a spectacular evening fireworks display.*

Orville felt terrible about Selfridge's death, but he did not lose his nerve. He spent seven weeks in the hospital, nursed by Katharine. Then the two of them sailed to France to join Wilbur. Orville knew that Wilbur was now famous, but he wasn't prepared for how great a celebrity his brother had become.

The whole of Europe was crazy about Wilbur. Every little thing that he did made headlines in the newspapers, and cartoonists loved to draw him, with his hawklike nose and bald head. People were amazed that he slept in the hangar with a mongrel dog he called Flyer. They were fascinated by his clothes—the dark suits and stiff collars and ties he wore every day, even when flying or working on the plane. The green cap he once wore was copied by the thousands and marketed as a "Veelbur."

The three Wrights spent several months in Europe, with the brothers flying before royalty, heads of state, and crowds of ordinary people, and signing several contracts to build planes. Then it was America's chance to honor its own.

(Opposite) Wilbur flies along the Hudson River from Governors Island to Grant's Tomb and back again, a total of almost 42 miles (68 km), on October 4, 1909. A canoe was fixed to the Flyer *to keep the plane afloat in case of an emergency water landing.*

On their return to Dayton in May 1909, Wilbur and Orville found themselves the stars of a huge celebration that lasted two days. Finally people had begun to realize the importance of what the brothers had accomplished. On October 4, Wilbur flew around the island of Manhattan before a million enraptured spectators. The Wrights were hailed as "The First Heroes of the New Century."

MAGNOLIA

EPILOGUE

The fields of Huffman Prairie fell away beneath them as the *Flyer* picked up speed and rose slowly into the air. It was May 25, 1910, and Orville's passenger was his father, eighty-one-year-old Bishop Milton Wright. An hour earlier, Wilbur and Orville had completed their one and only joint flight—something they had promised their father they would never do. Now the bishop himself was flying for the very first time. Orville worried that it would be too much for him. But as the bishop felt the rush of the air and the vibrations of the engine, he shouted in his son's ear, "Higher, Orville! Higher!"

Perhaps the bishop remembered that day more than thirty years ago when he threw a flying toy into the air to the delight of his two youngest sons, and now he marveled at how far they had come. Wilbur and Orville had founded the Wright Company of Dayton, Ohio in 1909, and they licensed their designs to manufacturing companies in Europe. These factories produced some of the world's first commercial aircraft. Orville trained pilots and organized flying exhibitions while Wilbur ran the business as company president. Wilbur's biggest worry was other companies trying to steal their inventions, and he was constantly in court trying to persuade judges to uphold their patent.

But the stress of all these legal battles broke Wilbur's health, and he fell sick with typhoid, like his brother had sixteen years earlier. He died on May 30, 1912, aged forty-five.

(Above) Workmen assemble Flyers *at the Wright Company's factory. (Left) The brothers on the steps of the rear porch of the Hawthorn Street house in June 1909. (Opposite) Orville takes his father up on his only flight. (Below and bottom) The Wright mansion today, and shortly after the family moved into the house in the spring of 1914. Bishop Wright is seated in the middle, with Katharine to his right, and Orville standing between them.*

"A short life," Bishop Wright wrote in his diary, "full of consequences. An unfailing intellect, imperturbable temper, great self-reliance, and as great modesty, seeing the right clearly, pursuing it steadfastly, he lived and died."

Orville carried on alone. Three years later, he sold the Wright Company and retired to his mansion in Dayton. He liked to drive his car fast (with the local police turning a blind eye) to work every day, where he would do research in his laboratory. His experiments helped develop the first automatic pilot and the wing flaps later used on dive bombers and the Space Shuttle. Orville died in 1948, having lived to see the jet plane and the atomic bomb. The world has moved faster and faster since Orville's time, but no one will ever forget that day in December 1903, when two brothers made a plane take off under its own power and fly through the air for the first time ever.

(Above) The Wright Brothers National Memorial at Kill Devil Hills was dedicated in 1932. The inscription reads: "In commemoration of the conquest of the air by the brothers Wilbur and Orville Wright. Conceived by genius. Achieved by dauntless resolution and unconquerable faith." (Inset) Stone markers show the distances of the Wright brothers' first flights.

IMPORTANT DATES

1867 ● Wilbur Wright is born (April 16).

1871 ● Orville Wright is born (August 19).

1878 ● Wilbur and Orville experiment with toy helicopters.

1885 ● Wilbur is injured playing ice hockey.

1886 ● Orville starts a printing business.

1888 ● Wilbur and Orville build a bigger press.

1889 ● Susan Wright dies.

● Brothers publish *The West Side News.*

1892 ● Wrights buy safety bicycles. December: They start their bicycle business.

1896 ● Wrights begin making their own bicycles.

● Orville becomes ill with typhoid.

● Otto Lilienthal dies in a glider crash.

1899 ● Printing shop is sold.

● Wilbur contacts the Smithsonian Institution for help with information on flight.

● Brothers make a biplane kite and test the wing-warping theory.

1900 ● Wrights fly their first glider at Kitty Hawk, North Carolina.

1901 ● Second glider does not perform as well. Wilbur and Orville conduct wind-tunnel tests.

1902 ● Brothers fly nearly 1,000 flights in their third glider at Kill Devil Hills, just south of Kitty Hawk.

1903 ● The Wrights build the *Flyer* and make first successful controlled powered flights in history.

1904 ● Wilbur and Orville build and fly the *Flyer II.*

1905 ● They build and fly the *Flyer III.*

1908 ● Wilbur demonstrates the Wright plane in France.

● At U.S. Army tests, Orville crashes and is injured. His passenger, Lt. Thomas Selfridge, is killed: the first fatality in airplane flying.

1909 ● The Wrights fly in Europe.

● They sell their first planes and the Wright Company is set up to build them.

● Dayton honors the Wrights.

● Wilbur gives public flying show at Hudson-Fulton Celebration in New York.

1912 ● Wilbur dies of typhoid (May 30), age forty-five.

1914–1918 ● World War I accelerates design and production of aircraft.

1915 ● Orville sells the business and retires.

1917 ● Bishop Wright dies.

1932 ● Memorial at Kitty Hawk is dedicated.

1939–1945 ● World War II speeds up further aircraft development.

1948 ● Orville dies (January 30), age seventy-six.

GLOSSARY

Biplane A plane or glider with two sets of wings, one above the other (double-decker). The Wrights' 1899 kite was a biplane (or box) kite.

Drag The friction between air and a moving plane, acting to hold the plane back.

Glider An unpowered plane.

Helicopter An aircraft that gets its lift from powered rotors (long narrow wings or blades). The first helicopters were actually toys from as long ago as the fourteenth century. They were powered by string and later rubber bands. The forerunner of the modern helicopter was developed in the late 1930s.

Horsepower A unit of power used when describing engines.

Lift The force that gives a plane its upward movement.

Muslin A durable plain-woven cotton fabric.

Safety bicycle The name given to the modern-style bicycle, with equal-sized wheels. It was called this because it was safer to ride than previous models.

Sateen A durable shiny cotton fabric.

Thrust The force that gives a plane forward movement.

Tuberculosis A disease affecting the lungs.

SELECTED BIBLIOGRAPHY

For young readers

The Wright Brothers by Quentin Reynolds (Random House, 1981)

The Wright Brothers: How They Invented the Airplane by Russell Freedman (Holiday House, 1991)

The Wright Brothers: The Story of the Struggle to Build and Fly the First Successful Aeroplane by Anna Sproule (Exley Publishers and Irwin, 1996)

For older readers and adults

The Bishop's Boys: A Life of Wilbur and Orville Wright by Tom Crouch (Norton, 1989)

How We Invented the Airplane: An Illustrated History by Orville Wright and edited by Fred C. Kelly (Dover, 1988)

Miracle at Kitty Hawk: The Letters of Wilbur and Orville Wright edited by Fred C. Kelly (Farrar, Straus & Giroux, 1951)

On Great White Wings: The Wright Brothers and the Race for Flight by Fred E. C. Culick and Spencer Dunmore (Airlife and Hyperion, 2001)

The Wright Brothers: A Biography by Fred C. Kelly (Harcourt, 1943). This biography was authorized by Orville Wright.

Web sites

Franklin Institute www.fi.edu/flights/first/intro.html

Henry Ford Museum www.hfmgv.org/exhibits/wright

National Air and Space Museum (a division of the Smithsonian Institution) www.nasm.edu

PBS www.pbs.org/wgbh/amex/wright/glider.html

Smithsonian Institution www.si.edu

Wright Brothers Aeroplane Company and Museum www.first-to-fly.com

Wright Brothers Special Collection at Wright State University www.libraries.wright.edu/special/wright_brothers

Commemorating the centennial of flight

www.aviation-worlds-fair.com/default.htm

www.centennialofflight.gov/1903.htm

www.flight100.org/history/wright.html

www.wrightflyer.org

PICTURE CREDITS

Every effort has been made to attribute correctly all material reproduced in this book. If any errors have unwittingly occurred, we will be happy to correct them in future editions.

All paintings are by David Craig unless otherwise stated. All archival photographs, unless otherwise stated, are from the Wright Brothers Collection at the Wright State University Special Collections and Archives. All diagrams are by Jack McMaster.

2: (bottom right) Northwind Picture Archives
6: (top) Peter Christopher © 2001; (center) Library of Congress; (bottom) Gaslight Advertising Archives
7: (top) Hulton Archive; (center) Image Select/Art Resource, NY
8: (top) Hulton Archive; (center) Image Select/Art Resource, NY; (bottom) Corbis/Magma
10: (left top, center, and bottom) Library of Congress
12: (top) Nick Engler/Wright Brothers Aeroplane Company; (bottom) Library of Congress
13: (top right) Library of Congress
15: ARC (Ames Research Center) AC99-003-4
18: Library of Congress
20–21: Library of Congress
23: (top) Bettmann/Corbis/Magma
24: (bottom) Mary Evans Picture Library
26: (top) John Provan (Private Collection)
29: (left center) Peter Christopher © 2001; (left bottom) Library of Congress
30: (inset and right) Peter Christopher © 2001

INDEX

First published in the United States by Crown Publishers, a division of Random House, Inc. 1540 Broadway, New York, New York 10036

CROWN and colophon are trademarks of Random House, Inc.

www.randomhouse.com/kids

Library of Congress Cataloging-in-Publication Data

Busby, Peter.
First to fly : how Wilbur & Orville Wright invented the airplane / by Peter Busby ; paintings by David Craig ; diagrams by Jack McMaster ; historical consultation by Fred E. C. Culick.
p. cm.
Summary: A look at the lives of the Wright brothers, from their childhood interest in flight, through their study of successful gliders and other flying machines, to their triumphs at Kitty Hawk and beyond.

Includes bibliographical references and index.

ISBN 0-375-81287-3 (trade hc)
ISBN 0-375-91287-8 (lib. bdg.)

1. Wright, Orville, 1871-1948—Juvenile literature. 2. Wright, Wilbur, 1867-1912—Juvenile literature. 3. Aeronautics—United States—Biography—Juvenile literature. [1. Wright, Orville, 1871-1948. 2. Wright, Wilbur, 1867-1912. 3. Aeronautics—Biography.] I. Craig, David, ill. II. McMaster, Jack, ill. III. Title.
TL540.W7 B88 2003
629.13'092'273—dc21
2002000849

Printed and bound in Malaysia
2002
1 3 5 7 9 10 8 6 4 2

Editorial Director: Hugh Brewster
Art Director: Gordon Sibley
Graphic Designer: Nathan Beyerle
Project Editor: Catherine Fraccaro
Consultants: Fred E.C. Culick and Nick Engler
Consulting Editor: Ian R. Coutts
Editorial Assistance: Nan Froman
Production Director: Susan Barrable
Production Manager: Donna Chong
Color Separation: Colour Technologies
Printing and Binding: Tien Wah Press

FIRST TO FLY: HOW WILBUR & ORVILLE WRIGHT INVENTED THE AIRPLANE was produced by Madison Press Books, which is under the direction of Albert E. Cummings.

Madison Press Books
1000 Yonge Street, Suite 200
Toronto, Ontario, Canada M4W 2K2